Jewels *from* Heaven

Corinne Mae Lindsay

Jewels from Heaven

Published by Corinne Mae Lindsay
Brisbane, Queensland, Australia

Edited by Steve Harris
Founder, Global Influencers www.globalinfluencers.org

Copyright © 2023 by Corinne Mae Lindsay
All Rights Reserved

ISBN   978-0-6450343-8-7 (paperback)

ISBN   978-0-6450343-9-4 (eBook)

This book or parts thereof may not be reproduced in any form, stored in a retrieval system, or transmitted in any form by any means - electronic, mechanical, photocopy, recording, or otherwise - without prior written permission of the publisher, except as provided by Australian copyright law.

Bible Versions Used

Unless otherwise indicated, all Scripture quotations are taken from the **New King James Version®**. Copyright © 1982 by Thomas Nelson. Used by permission. All rights reserved.

Amplified Bible (AMP)
Scripture quotations marked **(AMP)** are taken from the Amplified® Bible (AMP), Copyright © 2015 by The Lockman Foundation. Used by permission. www.Lockman.org

God's Word Translation (GW)
Scripture quotations marked **(GW)** are taken from the God's Word Translation. Copyright © 1995, 2003, 2013, 2014, 2019, 2020 by God's Word to the Nations Mission Society. All rights reserved.

New International Version (NIV)
Scripture quotations marked **(NIV)** are taken from the Holy Bible, New International Version®, NIV®. Copyright © 1973, 1978, 1984, 2011 by Biblica, Inc.™ Used by permission of Zondervan. All rights reserved worldwide. www.zondervan.com

The "NIV" and "New International Version" are trademarks registered in the United States Patent and Trademark Office by Biblica, Inc.™

New Living Translation (NLT)
Scripture quotations marked **(NLT)** are taken from the *Holy Bible*, New Living Translation, copyright © 1996, 2004, 2015 by Tyndale House Foundation. Used by permission of Tyndale House Publishers, Inc., Carol Stream, Illinois 60188. All rights reserved.

Foreword

A word was given to me in 1990 that God
was going to pour jewels into my hands.

This word was reaffirmed in 2002,
and I began to write down these jewels
from heaven, knowing that they would
be released in God's perfect timing..

This book, I believe,
is the fulfilment of those words.

I encourage you to read these words out loud
and be personally blessed with love, hope and joy.

In the Name of Jesus and for His glory.

Corinne Mae Lindsay
March 2023

Dedication

This book is dedicated to :-

Father God -
Who said "I AM your Father"
and has provided for me every day of my life.

Jesus -
Whose love overwhelms me
as we walk the journey of life together every day.

The Holy Spirit -
Who guides me in every way.

My wonderful children,
Kath and Adam,
whom I so dearly love.

My three amazing grandchildren,
Emily, Harry and Mark,
who bring me so much joy.

My dear sister, Carol, in Wisconsin.
I miss you, and I thank you for all the times,
even from far away, that you have been here for me.

and

To the memory of my late, loving husband Sno (Beresford) Lindsay.

I have been, and always will be, so blessed.

Acknowledgements

I acknowledge and thank God
for these special people :-

Brenda, who knows me so well,
who encourages me greatly
and is always there
with wisdom, laughter, and tears.

Lenore, we have shared our lives
for so many years.
What a blessing it has been.

Lois, who often disappears
with husband Vern to look after
a few thousand sheep in the outback.
Always glad to see her come back!

My dear friend Judy – we have been here
for each other for so long, and we have
such a precious friendship.

And dear Jan, who has blessed me
in so many ways over these years.

Steve Harris, my good friend
who encouraged me to put this book together.
Thank you, Steve, for all of your help and advice.

There are many more whose names should have been here.
I have been greatly blessed and I thank God so much
for all those He has put into my life.

Table of Contents

Foreword   iii
Dedication   iv
Acknowledgements   v

Part 1 - GOD'S GLORY

The Glory of God	3
Majesty	4
The Throne of Glory	5
Tiny Bells of Glory	6
God's Art	7
The Kaleidoscope of Heaven	8
The Keys of Heaven	10
The Tale of a Meteor	12
The Symphony of Heaven	13
God's Garden	14

Part 2 - JOY

A Pearl	21
Rushing Waters	22
The Day God Whispered on the Breeze	23
Butterfly Jazz	24
Fragrant Whispers of God's Flower Garden	25
The Crowns of Revelations	26
The Oil of Anointing	28
Walking With Jesus	29

Part 3 – LIFE

The Spheres of Life	33
The Beauty of Faith	34
Stop	35
Listen	36
Celestial Air	37
Tears of the Heart	38
What Is it That You Have ?	40

Part 4 - TRIALS

Sighs	45
Burden to Beauty	46
The Day God Spoke to Me	47
The Window in the Sky	48
God's Army	50
Rumbling Hooves	51

Part 5 - HOPE

The Winds of Faith	55
The Rock of Hope	56
Two Pieces of Wood	58
The Waters of Redemption	60
Two Gardens	61
Hope in the Middle of the Storm	64
Father, I Am Home – Yay !	65

Part 1
God's Glory

The Glory of God

The upper reaches of space
– where clouds move – dance !
– where angelic beings are continually spinning,
twisting, whirling - turning in the midst of God's glory.

All of this is recorded, told, and inscribed
in the Chronicles by celestial beings
– unending reports of the sights and sounds of heaven.

The great, continual expanding
of the no beginning – no end of the open heavens
– being controlled, formed, brought
into continually new beginnings
by the incredible awesomeness of power
from His open hand – expanding, changing,
adding new yet retaining the "old" firmament
that we can see – stationary – yet new coming into being
in far reaches of this universe.

We can only begin to see the everlasting power
of the weight of His untouchable awesome glory.

One day we will be in it
– dancing, whirling with the angels
over the endless clouds,
forming puffs of delight as we bask
in the awesome glory of our God.

***

The heavens declare the glory of God.
And the firmament shows His handiwork.
Psalm 19:1

Majesty

The sky will unfold
like a great ocean wave
as it travels across the universe
– breaking into its depth,
then soaring in His glory,
crashing again
as it is carried across
the never-ending ocean
of dominion and power.

Worship His Majesty.

To God be the glory !

***

To God our Saviour,
Who alone is wise,
Be glory and majesty,
dominion and power,
both now and forever.
Amen.
Jude 1:25

The Throne of Glory

To Him who sits on the throne

KADOSH KADOSH KADOSH

HOLY HOLY HOLY

To Him be glory forever.

Hands are held open to **YHWH**
in praise and worship
with blessing and honour
and glory and power
all around.

There is glory, glistening
from small golden leaves,
coming from and falling
all around the throne.

Golden oil is pouring
into open hands
- pouring out before us
- flowing all around us.

All for His glory !

The glory of Almighty God

El Shaddai

***

*... and behold, a throne set in heaven,
and One sat on the throne.*
Revelation 4:2

Tiny Bells of Glory

Under the blue sky and in the warm sunshine
I walk through a field
of beautiful flowers.

A summer shower,
being released from the confines
of its misty veil,
gently falls all around me,
as tiny bells of the purest liquid
release their beauty,
caught by the rays of the sun,
bathing all in their splendour.

I stop - I listen
- raising my face to this
- a cascade of heavenly glory,
letting myself be refreshed
in this special moment.

I hear His love falling around me -
causing the beauty of the flowers
to release their fragrance
as they rejoice along with the sound
of a thousand tiny bells
of softly falling rain.

***

You visit the earth and water it;
You make it soft with showers.
Psalm 65:9a, 10b

God's Art

When walking through the countryside one day ...

... I came across a large field
of brilliant yellow blossoms
and watched in amazement
as it rose as a painting of beauty,
lifting into the sky above.

Butterflies joyously flutter in and out of the field
honouring the Creator who placed them there;

Talons of the wings of angels touching the blooms
as they come flying past, causing the blossoms to shake
with gentle joy at being part of the world, He has made.

Such pleasure as He watches with delight what He is doing.

And the field of blossoms dances with joy as it continues
to rise and join the wonders of the beauty of creation.

As I watch I see the Artist's painting of colour sailing
through the air- with multicoloured rainbows encircling
the blossoms in their beauty – framing the work of art.

The field becomes
a framed picture of glory
that hangs on the walls of space,
creating divine displays of art by the Creator
Who brings a heavenly art gallery
into the universe.

***

*The heavens declare the glory of God,
and the sky displays what his hands have made.*
Psalm 19:1 (GW)

The Kaleidoscope of Heaven

I woke with excitement to a new day,
wondering what I will hear and see.

Maybe I will hear words that drip with honey !

Or see colours that will bombard the sky
as I look upward into the heavens,
seeing the sun lighting up the waking universe
with its rays heralding the birth of a new day.

Colours – LORD, that You send forth through the clouds
- they sail past like giant clipper ships
with sails unfurled, blowing in the wind...

Then seeing others– dark - foreboding yet bringing joy
as they release their waters upon the parched earth.
And we see the colours of a rainbow joining together
as they bring its beauty into the midst of the storm.

As the storm passes, the clouds freely race away,
bringing us back to the awesome sunrise into a clear blue sky.

Meanwhile, the clipper ships continue on their way
across the heavens with the wind taking them
on their journey throughout the day,
until the time comes when the sun slowly goes down,
and a quietness fills the world.

At that moment comes the unbelievable sunset
– paintings from the very hand
of the Master Artist, God Himself,
bringing the beauty that comes as the colours of the sky
turn into a painting that takes our breath away,
as they fulfil the desire and love of the Creator to bless us.

And as the sun goes further on its way,
the sky continues its part of this changing vision,
as we watch the coming of a star-studded universe
as the blackness of the night settles in.

Once again, God waves His hand,
and the night sky bursts into being,
and for our joy and pleasure we see stars,
galaxies, and the moon, and in the blink of an eye,
a comet shoots across the vast sphere,
only to disappear as fast as it came.

A sky with no ending,
showing us the beauty placed there
by the wave of God's hand.

Thank You, Almighty God,
for all that You have given us.

How great You are !

***

*In the beginning
God created
the heavens
and the earth.*
Genesis 1:1

*The heavens declare
the glory of God;
the skies proclaim
the work of His hands.*
Psalm 19:1 (NIV)

The Keys of Heaven

One evening as I looked up, I saw a massive explosion of what looked like millions of small white, rectangular flat objects pushing their way into the far reaches of the sky.

Then all at once, another explosion – as strong as the first but this time forcing millions of black partly rounded, smaller rectangular-shaped objects to go forth, also pushing their way into the reaches
of the sky.

What *are* these ? As I watched they are manoeuvring into some form of order. Looking closer I realized they were becoming the keyboards of pianos - beautiful ivory keys for the lower keyboard, and black onyx keys for the upper with their smooth, rounded beauty - but of all different lengths.

All preparing to become the keys of a keyboard ! Not just 88 keys. I can't count them ! There were millions ! The ivory and onyx forms are about to become the keys of the *keyboards of heaven*!

Yet another explosion pushed out long sheets of what looked like white paper – these were also rectangular and flying at high speed across the sky - yet keeping in their own space ... then settling down quietly – waiting.

I couldn't see how long these were –but realized they were varied lengths of keyboards ... the boards waiting for the arriving keys!

I was mesmerized, watching to see what was going to happen next.

As I watched, the keys came flying through the air towards the keyboards, taking their places and then stopping. There was total silence. Millions of them waiting ... perfectly still in anticipation of what was coming.

All at once, more sheets of again what looked like white paper exploded in the heavenlies, all different sizes but with the same carvings on them. I realized they were completed sheets of music with the upper and lower clefs but with many lines. And all at once they, too, came to a standstill - now waiting - waiting for the notes.

By this time I am just standing in awe after watching the sky exploding into something only God can do.

The scene is now complete. The keyboards are ready.
The sheet music is ready....
But there is something missing !
Where are the notes ?

The notes are silently rushing through the heavenlies, straining to get to their sheets – then hovering over them – I can hear them, restless, but I can't see them. They are there, but not visible to the naked eye.

They, too, are waiting.

And then I heard a wind come racing across the universe . All at once they were here ! Angels ! Millions of angels ! They are flying to the keyboards. An awesome sight !

As they arrive, I can hear the notes drop into place and these heavenly beings settle over their keyboards, and with their talons at the end of their wingtips touching the keys, they begin to play from the sheets of music.

One angel per keyboard ? No ! Many !

What is happening ? The excitement is overwhelming !

Then the whole universe exploded, and I was in awe
at what I was seeing and hearing.

The moment a note was played, it became an astonishing colour never before seen, and with a sound never before heard. Every note had a new and different colour and sound! As the angels played, every note soared throughout the universe, causing these magnificent sounds and sights to fill the entire sky.

It was a glorious piano recital from the Keyboards of Heaven !
It was a cacophony of heavenly music and colour ...
Praising Almighty God, the Creator !

And I stood amazed!

***

Praise God in His sanctuary; praise Him in His mighty firmament.
Psalm 150:1

Be exalted, O God, above the heavens.
Psalm 108:5

The Tale of a Meteor

A song of heaven soars
as its notes rise and fall across the skies
in beautiful undulating crescendos
of sounds and colours
never before seen or heard.

From out of nowhere,
a meteor passes through,
its tail leaving a sparkling residue,
bringing startling harmony to the song
as it races across the heavenlies.

It continues fleeing into the darkness
until it comes into the soaring notes
and colours of yet another song of heaven
– coming out of nowhere yet everywhere.

The meteor's notes once again bring their harmony
as its tail passes through this song and into the heavens,
once again joining in these never-ending melodies.

This beauty of the mystifying sights and sounds of heaven
are coming from the very throne room of God,
a gift given by Him who sits upon the throne,
to bless us all as He shows us His glory.

How great is our God !

***

"The skies sent out a sound ..."
Psalm 77:17

The Symphony of Heaven

Angels running across the strings of a harp -

… the smooth tones of clarinets sensing the change in the atmosphere, and then the sound of flutes sending their satin notes racing across the skies in anticipation of what is coming.

Flashes of lightning strike the air around them as the piccolo reaches its height of rising notes – like a shard of ice striking its invisible target.

Clarinets stretching as the lightning begins to speed across the sky colliding with the coming low rumble of thunder – the timpani quietly sending out their measured muted beats across the restless sky,

Droplets of rain begin to fall as the snare drums begin their ever-increasing rhythms in anticipation of the coming storm. and then the universe is shattered by the bass drum releasing its energy – its thunder that causes the heavens to shake wildly with repeated choruses, until it melts away like the sun hitting a shard of ice as the storm disappears into the atmosphere.

In its place come soft winds as violins bring their silk-lined sounds into the refreshed heavens – with cellos and deep bass releasing their throaty tones joining the rhythm of the strings that reach across the sky.

The oboe and bassoon insert their mysterious sounds into this cacophony that is stretching across the heavens that are groaning and stretching like an expectant mother, as all heaven awaits the birth of another storm that releases new life into the atmosphere above and around us.

***

And I heard a sound from heaven,
like the roar of rushing waters
and like a loud peal of thunder.

The sound I heard was like that
of harpists playing their harps.
Revelation 14:2

God's Garden

I have a little garden …

… that has a fishpond with two goldfish and three rocks in it.

It made me think about **God's garden.**

Come on a journey with me.

God's garden ponds are the oceans and the seas…underwater mountain ranges…rivers.. reefs with their beautifully coloured fish and corals, and also there are the drab browns of the not-so-so-beautiful catfish !

The giant whales, dolphins, sharks, jellyfish, the big cod, and the tiniest fish that you can scarcely see with the naked eye are all in His ponds.

***

You may have a rock garden by your home. Little garden lizards running around, small plants, ground covers. Is *that* a snake ?

God's rock gardens are the mountains…where a carpet of leaves and twigs cover the ground under the trees at the foot of the mountains.

As you go higher, the way becomes strewn with rocks and rocky outcrops - a place where mountain goats scamper and mountain lions prowl - where the tree line disappears as you reach the top of this great rock garden.

And in the very high places, you are surrounded by a mantle of pure white, as the snow gives a covering from the hand of the Almighty – shimmering in the sunlight – dazzling your eyes !

***

My flower garden has a few rose and geranium bushes, and a butterfly comes to have a rest.

God's flower garden is all the valleys, the meadows, the fields of the world covered in wildflowers…fields of golden buttercups; blue cornflowers reflecting the sky; acres and acres of tulips of every colour.

There are roses everywhere, growing to their full beauty, their fragrance drifting on the breeze.

Butterflies by the thousands dancing from flower to flower, as do the amazing tiny Hummingbirds hanging in the air doing 80 wing beats a second as they drink lantana nectar.

***

We see fountains in the park and in the gardens.

God's fountains are the majestic waterfalls – Victoria Falls in Africa, Niagara Falls, the falls we catch glimpses of as we drive through our rain forests and there are the waterfalls never seen by man – put there and seen only by God.

As the waters of Niagara *fall*, so it is when He opens the heavens to release the waters it holds, as He looks after His garden to keep it refreshed and cared for, for us.

***

Many of us have a shade tree in our yard.

God's shade tree is the canopy of trees covering the earth; the beautiful jacaranda that we see in the Spring, with its clouds and carpets of lavender wherever we look; an avenue of Poincianas with their red or orange flowers sitting atop the lush green of their foliage. The Eucalyptus shows us God's love as we sit under them and just rest. The fragrance of the cedars. Others put on brilliant Autumn colours heralding the coming winter.

We may have an orange or lemon tree outside our door. *God's orchard* reaches from one end of the earth to the other; from lychees to apples; from figs to cherries; from dates to oranges. And abundant, mouth-watering baskets of fruit for us to eat.

***

In our garden, we may have honeyeaters or parrots that sit in our trees.

God's garden has a full choir that sings continually – reaching all around the earth. From robins and larks to the bellbirds and magpies; from doves to the birds of paradise, yes the honey-eaters and parrots, and also to the everywhere crows ! Each brings their own song causing a symphony of praise to their Creator.

***

And I have a dog that roams in my garden. Many of us do – or maybe a cat.

In **God's garden** roam the brumbies of Fraser Island -   buffalo, once again on the plains of America.

The majestic elephants and lions of Africa. Koalas sitting in the trees and kangaroos hopping under them, and monkeys swinging in them. He has given us the pleasure to enjoy the animals who live in His garden all around the world.

And lastly, we have a 24-hour light show. Our garden is often caught up in the reflections from the lights that are all around us – the lights of the world – glaring – from white to all colours – at times flashing for effect.

But from our gardens, we can see that **God's lights are endless** – the effect, endless. At dawn we wake to the display of beauty unequalled in any light show man may try to put on.

The *crack* of dawn is just that, as the rays of the sun force their way through the opening of the night, and from our garden we see the rays reach with their fingers into the heavenlies. Shades of pink, purple, and yellow light up the sky as God paints for us His picture of the new day.

And as the sun climbs, the sky is bathed in blue with whispers of clouds that sail across this unending space all day, until He is painting another masterpiece for us. This time a panoramic display of breathtaking beauty as He covers us in the folds of the coming night with shades of gold that extends to pale pink, at times a brilliant orange that takes your breath away.

As it fades, the shadows of the night are waiting to enter and then the blackness of the sky is alive with billions of tiny lights…sparkling, twinkling, filling our eyes everywhere we look – with the moon, seeming to just hang there as it follows the guidance of the Creator. And we become star gazers as we look at the Universe He has given us. Even when the sun is bright, they are there but we cannot see them. We can never get away from the stars…

God is everywhere. He has given us beauty on this earth for our eyes to see – sounds to hear – fragrances to enjoy. But we can go through life not seeing or experiencing these things. But we know they are there. And as like the stars, He is always there -He never leaves us although at times we can't see Him.

If we close our eyes to God, we are burying ourselves in a hole – in a dark, ugly hole. There are times when we feel like we are in that place. Life isn't easy but don't put the cover over 'it. Instead, look up, grab His hand and climb out of it and live in the vibrant and beautiful garden He has given you.

When God created the earth, He wanted to share it with someone.

He wanted someone to talk to. And He wanted to give it to someone.

So He created Adam – and gave the garden to him. They walked and talked together.

Then God gave Adam a mate so he would have company too.

So much joy !

But Adam and Eve broke His law and had to leave the garden – they were made to leave God's presence. And that is what would happen to us if it hadn't been for Jesus.

God wanted us to live in His garden with Him,
to talk with Him, to walk with Him.

So He sent His own Son to die for each and every one of us – so that once again we can come to Him – and when the time comes, walk with Him in His garden.

God Has given us everything. And that includes His beautiful garden.

Open our eyes, Lord, so we can see – can hear - can taste, and can smell the fragrance that is there - *the fragrance of Jesus.*

***

¹ Praise the Lord!
Praise the Lord from the heavens;
Praise Him in the heights!
³ Praise Him, sun and moon;
Praise Him, all you stars of light!
⁴ Praise Him, you heavens of heavens,
And you waters above the heavens!

⁷ Praise the Lord from the earth,
you great sea creatures and all the depths;
⁸ Fire and hail, snow and clouds;
Stormy wind, fulfilling His word;
⁹ Mountains and all hills; fruitful trees and all cedars;
¹⁰ Beasts and all cattle; creeping things and flying fowl;
¹² Both young men and maidens;
Old men and children.

¹³ Let them praise the name of the Lord,
For His name alone is exalted;
His glory is above the earth and heaven.
Psalm 148:1,3-4,7-10,12-13

Part 2
Joy

A Pearl

I saw a large group of people …

… young and old - running
- skipping down streets
that were leading to a country road.

They were excited and in such a hurry
- happy and full of joy !

Then I looked down the road,
at the fields where there were many hills,
and people were flooding over them
- coming from every direction,
running across the fields towards the road.

What is happening ?

What is over there ?

I looked down the road
and saw a huge PEARL rolling along,
almost bouncing over the road,
and all these people were running after it.

Such excitement - such joy !

And then - all at once they stopped !

The PEARL was gone !

And there was **JESUS** standing in their midst !

Laughing – happy - dancing and having
a wonderful time with the children, with all the people.

There was such joy !

What an awesome sight !

***

"..a single pearl of great price."
Matthew 13:46a (AMP)

Rushing Waters

Oh – how I yearn for more of Your beautiful words.

Words that roar through my thoughts
like the rushing waters of a cool mountain stream
– over rocks and through endless twists and turns
- at times roaring along their seemingly endless journey,
only to hit a submerged rock and roar back
to where they came from - then continuing their journey
down the path You have made for them.

So it is with my thoughts – they rush through my mind
– exciting, loving the freedom I have in You.

Then I hit a submerged rock
– and I fall over it, arms flailing
– out of control and going in a direction
that doesn't go anywhere.

Then I come rushing back
and once again continue this journey with You,
Rejoicing in the rush as the Holy Spirit
reveals more of You to me.

Harmless bumps – teaching me more
- the constant, clear, sparkling waters
that never stop running and that
carry me on this remarkable journey
that You have made for me.

※※※

His voice was like the sound of many waters.
Ezekiel 43:2b

The Day God Whispered on the Breeze

We went for a walk, my friend and I.

She said *"come see my land"*
and we strolled along the way.

We were soon walking over the brown ground dotted
with little clusters of pink as the lantana spread wide its fingers.

The eucalyptus trees are tall and alive with birds
calling with their songs – never stopping.

The kookaburras are laughing with joy as they joined the others
and praised the One who had made them.

As we walked on, I could see a change as we approached
the narrow beginning of a gully. Balga Grass plants
are scattered everywhere; their special uniqueness
giving us pleasure wherever we looked.

We walked further into the narrow confines.

All at once I could sense it:
the presence of the Creator in all that surrounded us.

Then silence came - I stood there – scarcely able to breathe;
in awe of being in the presence of God.

A slight sound was heard in the midst of the silence
– a soft rustle of wind - that came from nowhere
– yet from everywhere.

Drinking in where I was and what was happening,
I realized it was the day when God came in the wind
to my friend and I.

It was the day that **God whispered on the breeze.**

✼✼✼

Who walks on the wings of the wind.
Psalm 104:3b

Butterfly Jazz

Walking along in the countryside one day,
I came across a field of brilliant flowers
and watched in amazement as they began to move
in rhythm along with "jazz dancing" butterflies
who were going along for the ride.

They were joyously fluttering in and out of the field,
dancing to "angelic jazz music" that seemed to drop
on them as the flowers rose to the open heaven.

The angels entered the scene, watching with laughter,
the country field filled with music and dancing flowers,
joyfully moving to the jazz rhythm of the butterflies.

Soon they had to leave, so with the talons on their wingtips
brushing over the music-ridden blooms, they flew over the flowers
with speeds that resembled a space race - leaving the flowers
shaking with joy in excitement over what was happening.

Their shaking caused them to scatter across the skies,
with the dancing butterflies joining in as the flowers became
an explosion of colour that rocked the universe
- with the angels coming back and trying to catch the dancing flowers
and their butterflies, to bring some "order" into this hilarious show
of jumping jazz in the heavenlies !

Almighty God was laughing,
as He watched the 'Butterfly Jazz'.

***

A time to weep
and a time to laugh
a time to mourn
and a time to dance.
Ecclesiastes 3:4

Fragrant Whispers
of God's Flower Garden

His garden – not ours

Walking past what seems to be an especially beautiful flower garden - I pause, sensing something is different.

It is covered with dozens of various flowers in bud – ready to burst into full beauty at any moment...

But I am aware of not just the beautiful colour of the growing buds, but the seemingly *coloured fragrances* that are seeping out from this mass variety of blooms.

Yes, blooms give their fragrance - but these are still closed buds.

As their fragrances force their way through the maze of petals, they gently rise in their heaviness as they are wisps of scents of the coming heavy beauty preparing the way.

They are changing the atmosphere in preparation for the coming glory.

Fragrant colours of a whisper - all creating a silent cacophony of fragile mixed scents of beauty, rising from the cradles of their straining buds ...

... rising gently until the groaning fullness of the blooms cannot hold back any longer - and now, the fragrances explode in their fragility, as they send their beauty into the atmosphere - as the following blooms erupt into the fullness of their beauty ... being carried along, on the whispers of their fragrances.

A fleeting moment as one walks past the garden – that brings a smile as you walk through this garden of awesome beauty and fragrance, that is being watched over by their Creator.

A realm of awesome fragrant beauty.

Only God ...

***

"The LORD GOD planted a garden ..."
Genesis 2:8a

The Crowns of Revelation

I have just walked out into my front garden and looked
at my two frangipani trees. Winter has passed
and they have come out of their hibernation,
waking to a new day, a new season.

And a new day and a new season for us with Jesus !

The trees are coming alive with clumps of buds appearing
on the tops of their stems, green leaves surrounding them
– protecting them from any unwanted bugs.

Just as Jesus protects us as we grow more and more in Him.

As the straight flower stems grow, they shrug off
the remainder of the winter months and every day
brings them closer to the day they open and slowly become
gloriously coloured petals of perfect form.

The result of the Holy Spirit.

The green leaves completing their time of protection, now open,
bowing in their place - symbolizing the twenty-four elders
who are celestial representatives of all the redeemed,
and who are seated around the throne
with crowns of gold on their heads.

As we make ready for what is to come.

The stems, standing at attention at the base of the flowers,
from pollination to the crown, are themselves representing
the angelic hosts of heaven - physically protecting
these special buds as they make their way to their destiny.

God's angels who protect us.

These protected flower buds look like the tiny tips of crowns,
rising from their protective covering, each one, in time,
opening into the fullness of their beauty.

One at a time we are being prepared.

Crowns of loveliness in colour,
a pleasure to touch,
and a delightful fragrance,
all reflecting
the beauty of their Maker.

What we have to look forward to !

And so we thank our Creator God,
who has redeemed us
and given us so much beauty,
who watches over us
every day of our lives,
and who has made us who we are.

And we rejoice in what He has promised us
- crowns of glory and honour before Him,
and crowns of victory and joy.

Thank You, Jesus !

***

*Around the throne
were twenty-four thrones,
and on the thrones,
I saw twenty-four elders sitting,
clothed in white robes;
and they had crowns of gold on their heads.*
Revelation.4:4

*You have made him a little lower than the angels;
You have crowned him with glory and honour.*
Hebrews .2:7

*Do not forget to entertain strangers, for by so doing,
some have unwittingly entertained angels.*
Hebrews 13:2

The Oil of Anointing

Jesus, Yeshua, who was and is the Messiah ...

... The Promised One – The Anointed One.

The most holy anointing oil was poured on Jesus by Mary.

A special oil that would be used once – only once.

Preparing Him for what was to come. And what we use now to bring to His gift of salvation, love, healing, and joy to those around us.

Droplets of pure gold oil are falling all around
– they are the oil of joy – sparkling like the sun on the sea;
but these fill the air – droplets all over reaching to the ground.

Oh, such beauty, such joy, such purity. It is dazzling.
I have to squint as I look at them – all around – they are everywhere !

And there are people everywhere ! - laughing – dancing
- hugging each other – arms raised as they praise God the Father
- Almighty God - YHWH the great I AM - praising JESUS!

And Jesus, now I see You there in the midst of us ...
... laughing and laughing ! Your arms reaching up
in pure, unrestrained joy to Your Father.

Oh Lord, the preciousness of anointing oil.
Let me never take this lightly again.

***

"Then Mary took about a pint of pure nard, an expensive perfume; she poured it on His feet of Jesus and wiped His feet with her hair."
John 12:3 (NIV)

"You (Jesus) have loved righteousness and delighted in integrity and virtue and have hated lawlessness. Therefore, God has anointed You with the oil of exultant joy and gladness above and beyond Your companions.
Hebrews. 1:9 (AMP)

Walking With Jesus

For we walk by faith, not by sight.
2 Corinthians 5:7

We walk together, You and I, dear Jesus.

We come to a fork in the path.

"Which way should we go, Jesus ?"

"This way", He says.

"My way."

And we step onto this path that is full of cracks
- some small, some large, and some deep.

"What are these cracks, Lord ?"

*"They are the results of lives
going through trials and temptations"*,
He says.

These are things that cause us to stumble
- some small - just a hiccup in life.
Others that caused us to trip are deep
- but then we continue on.

There are days when we have fallen
because of circumstances that are beyond
what we can take, can handle, and can control.

Yet we have gotten the strength to rise up
and get out of it, leaving behind a scar,
but one healed over with only a faint crack among the others,
leaving a beautiful carving,
etched into the path we are now on.

And we continue walking His Way
- past massive fields of flowers
- kaleidoscopes of colour seemingly waving in the gentle breeze,
lightly bowing as we pass by, under the branches of trees
nodding to their Creator as we walk underneath them.

Our path begins to slant downward, bringing us
to a deep, quiet valley - a change in the atmosphere.

Where is He taking me ?

There are scattered rocks - some small – some huge.

Boulders are all around us – yet there are small touches
of beautiful flowers peeking out from between and behind them.

"What are these, Jesus ?"

"These are your walk of life.

*I will always be with you
as the trials of life try to trip you,
but I AM always in the middle of them with you !*

You will never walk alone."

I look up from the valley
to the majestic mountains that lie ahead.

"What are these ?" I ask.

"Those are for another day", He replies.

And I continue walking with Jesus.

※※※

*For He Himself has said,
"I will never leave you nor forsake you."*
Hebrews 13:5b

Part 3
Life

The Spheres of Life

I saw a huge **black** sphere in the heavens
- a place of pain – dark - almost foreboding.

As I watched I saw a brilliant white sphere
rising from its base – from the darkness,
rising **light** - rising with its rays
exploding across the heavens
- reaching into **light** the spheres of darkness
- exploding with majesty into every sphere,
and bringing **light** into the darkness
- bringing life out of death.

Jesus is the **light,**
His **light** penetrating the darkness
of our soul, our sin – bringing LIFE,
Exploding in overwhelming rays of love
into our very being as He destroys the darkness in us
with unbelievable power and replaces it
with His everlasting love.

His rays are now exploding from
us as we carry His **light,**
breaking through every spot of darkness
– freeing us, as we are now carried
on His rays of forgiveness – hope - LOVE,
as we now are reaching out to others
with the rays of life that He has given us.

***

Arise, Shine; for your light has come!
And the glory of the LORD is risen upon you.
For behold, the darkness shall cover the earth.

And deep darkness the people;
but the LORD will arise over you.
And His glory will be seen upon you.
Isaiah 60:1-2 (NKJV)

The Beauty of Faith

A Rose Bud - A Growing Faith

We look at a beautiful rose bud's perfection in detail.

Each petal tightly enfolds another, keeping the inside
of the bud safe, and protecting it until it is time.

The delicate fragrance hints at what is to come.

At the right moment, the bud unfolds its protecting petals,
becoming an open vision of perfection.

But oh ! Look ! There is a small blemish.
It isn't quite the flawless creation God had planned it to be.

Time goes on with petals no longer protecting but now completing
the full-blown beauty of the rose – the fragrance overwhelming !

It's miniscule flawed beauty going out
to touch others, and heralding

The Open Rose - A Grown Faith

Our faith is like this.
Like a rosebud - beautiful, fragrant but not yet complete.

As our spiritual lives grow we are like the rose,
Opening our hearts to become
the creation God created us to be.

Our perfect form, although marred by sin,
still carries the fragrance and beauty
we were created to be,
taking the presence, forgiveness,
and love of Jesus to all around us.

***

*... and the desert shall rejoice and blossom as the rose;
It shall blossom abundantly and rejoice,
even with joy and singing."*
Isaiah 35:1b

Stop

Almighty God, I hear You in the sound of the sea.

It is constant – never ceasing – unable to be stopped.
And I see You as I watch the lava flowing
from its tube – racing - destroying everything
in its path - unable to be stopped.

The only way they would be stopped is if You would
speak the word "STOP !" –and they would be still.

Almighty God - You could speak out the word "STOP"
and all creation would cease to exist.

Yet You see the tiniest creature – each grain of sand
– each dew drop and every tear that falls
from the eye of every person on this earth.
You hear each heartbeat - each thought
as though spoken aloud – oh my Lord.

You don't say STOP to any of these
- but You reach out and touch
all that You have made – and You are with us
every moment of our lives.

And in the midst of our stumbles – or falls
– You never give up on us.

Yes, we do things we shouldn't, and we have to stop.
You know this because You are always here.
Yet you don't put your hand up and say "STOP".
You just wait patiently until we see our failings and
stop them ourselves with the wisdom that You have given us.

And we praise Your Name and wait
for the day that comes when You **will** say STOP !

And Jesus comes for us.

Such love, You have for us, LORD.

***

*The fountains of the deep and the windows of heaven
were also stopped, and the rain from heaven was restrained."*
Genesis 8:2

Listen

As the quietness of the air is broken

by the rumblings of distant thunder,
the leaves on the trees rustle with
the whispers of breeze heralding the coming storm.

So it will be when Yeshua Hamaschiah,
Jesus the Messiah, returns.

The rumbles of the hooves of the horses of His angelic army
vibrate across the heavens as they sense what is coming and
the whispers of the Holy Spirit that move across the earth
as He speaks in increasing urgency of His coming.

We rush here and there -
"What should I do ? Where will I go ?"

STOP ! Stop and listen !
Listen to His whispers - whispers that bring hope,
forgiveness, joy, and a love far greater than any love
that you have ever known in your life.

For those who have never known love, be encouraged !
He will envelop you with His perfect love.
A love so dear that *He died for you* !

And He is coming for you – for all who believe in Him,
Coming to take you to His home, His heavenly Kingdom
where we will live for all eternity.

Take heed of the rumbling and the whispers.
These are heralding the return of the Lord Jesus.
Believe and LISTEN !

All in Almighty God's time.

***

*For God so loved the world that He gave His only begotten Son,
that whosoever believes in Him should not perish but have everlasting life.*
John 3:16

Celestial Air

What is celestial air ?
It is the breath of life !

Each breath I take brings air into me
- into my lungs that give me life.

But LORD, Your celestial air gives me a different life
- a life led by You showing me who You are
– breathing a new realm into me, with You.

Breathing holy, celestial air into my lungs
gives me a life beyond my understanding.

This is the realm of the Spirit.
Trusting in the Creator, I soar with Him,
receiving thoughts that are higher
than the highest wave on the sea,
or the highest mountain, or the highest cloud.

It is the celestial air that cleanses my very being.
Celestial air brings into me a life that takes my breath away
in the awesomeness of who You are.

This celestial air brings the sensation of Your being **in** me
– I can feel this, Jesus. I can feel a presence inside me
that goes beyond any human feeling I have.
The feeling of Your presence being one with me.
How awesome that is. How awesome You are.
I am humbled that You would do this to, in, and for me.

And in time to come, I will be with You
in the celestial air of love.
Oh, the awesomeness of Who You are
– breathing into us the love of our God.

※※※

*And the LORD God formed man of the dust of the ground
and breathed into his nostrils the breath of life.*
Genesis 2:7b

... and the God who holds your breath in His hand ...
Daniel 5:23c

Tears of the Heart

I listen to the drops of rain falling gently,
steadily, seemingly never to stop.

I sit quietly, a calmness all around me,
yet my heart silently weeps
with tears that fall as gently
and as steadily as the rain.

It weeps for the wrenching apart
of a friendship born in God's love.

I am sorry, God, for the hurt I have caused.

I pray with all my heart my friend finds peace and forgiveness
for the pain - that the resentment will pass.

Oh God, how *I* hurt too.

How my whole being cried out until like a dam,
the torrent burst over the top
and there was nothing to stop it.

And it swept over those in its path
destroying the fragility of a friendship.

Father, we are to strive daily after You.

But I fall, I stumble, I run into walls,
and yes, I run into people.

But I try, God. I really try.
And I know You are there to forgive.

To reach out Your hand, and say
"It's ok. I know how hard it is."

Help me to see others,
to be sensitive to what they are saying,
to be quiet in understanding.

As the rain continues to fall,
it nourishes the earth.

And new growth groans
- as does a woman in childbirth
as new life burst forth.

As the tears of my heart fall,
let them not disappear as a morning mist,
but let them grow in me Your wisdom,
and Your love - as painful as it may be.

Holy Spirit, nourish the love of Jesus in me.

A love that is strong enough
to understand my weakness,
and the weaknesses of others.

Because it is through weakness
that we become strong.

Only through You, Lord Jesus.

My love is for You, Father God.

I know you have forgiven me,
and I ask You to please help me
to forgive those who were,
and yes, are unable to see my pain.

So, Father God,
as the sad gentleness of the rain falls,
it is bringing newness of life.

Help me to learn
through these
tears of my heart.

Wash away my pain
and bring to me acceptance of changes
in the pathway of my life.

May I always hear Your voice
as I strain to listen - above the rain.

***

I have heard your prayer; I have seen your tears.
2 Kings 20:5b

What Is It That You Have ?

As I was out walking, I was thinking about You, God.

You created everything. You looked and saw that all was good.

And then You created man and woman to live in this wonderful world.
They ended up disobeying You, so You sent Your Son, Jesus Christ
to die for us, to save all of us from our sin.

And though we are forgiven, we still live in a world
that is lost and crying out for You. It is a world in great need.

And there is no doubt that You have many ways
of reaching out to those who live in it.

You are our Shepherd, and the blessings you have given us
as we have followed You, are awesome.

You care about our every need.

You take us into delightful places of rest and restoration.

You lead us along a safe path and come after us should we ever stray from it.

We thank You for touching us in so many different ways, God.

You have set a table before us that is also
a foreshadowing of a fantastic marriage feast to come.

We have the Holy Spirit who shows us new things,
and teaches us so many things from God.

He opens a whole new way of understanding.

It is no wonder that we can say 'my cup runneth over'
as we live in Your grace.

And so, you anoint our head with oil.

An anointing oil we have.
But this oil is different.
Its fragrance is different.
It is like a perfume.

As I walk on, I sense something following me.

It doesn't leave me.
It stops when I stop;
it moves when I move.

What is it ?

Then I remember the words You gave us – gave *'me'* - gave *'you'*
- *"Surely goodness and mercy shall follow me all the days of my life."*
I look back to the time when Jesus Christ came
to fulfill Your plan for those You have called by name.

Jesus, You are the source of God's *goodness and mercy* to us.
The Word says, *"goodness and mercy* shall follow me".
This means it is behind us.

But in order for this to happen,
'goodness and mercy' *have to be on us !*

My thoughts move to perfume.
We spray perfume on our body meaning it is on us,
and as we walk along, the fragrance flows from us
on to those who are behind us.

So it is with *goodness and mercy* – all that Jesus is
– flows onto those behind us as we walk on the journey
You have for us. We are taking Your blessings to those behind!

Jesus, I pray I will never forget that I am carrying Your blessings,
so that others will sense the *goodness and mercy* that You have
for them as I walk past them in my daily life. That the scent
of Your *goodness and mercy* will touch them and cause them to say,

"What was that ?"

And then to ask,

"What is it that you have ?"

***

*"Surely goodness and mercy shall follow me all the days of my life;
and I will dwell in the house of the LORD forever.'"*
Psalm 23:6

Part 4
Trials

Sighs

May my sighs be heard throughout the heavens.

My cries are unable to be spoken out loud
- so they are spoken through my sighs.

Silent weeping
– roaring through the heavenlies
– sighs pleading in hope
– the hope that comes from You, O God.

Sighs that You understand
– Your Father's heart reaching out
to the one from whom they are pouring out.

You are their only hope
– but they turn their head.
Yet, You turn Yours toward them
in encompassing, forgiving love.

Enemy tendrils try to reach them,
but they can't touch them !

There is a barrier of safety around them.

Thank You, Jesus !

Help them to "see" You.
It is just You and them.

I can do nothing but praise You.
My sighs have turned into a voice of praise
– sounding across the clouds
to Him Who was, Who is, and Who is to come.

***

*"And the ransomed of the LORD shall return and come
to Zion singing with everlasting joy on their heads.
They shall obtain joy and gladness and sorrow
and sighing shall flee away."*
Isaiah .35:10

Burden to Beauty

Help, Father.

I just can't keep carrying this.
Please help me !

I'm carrying such hurt
- such pain - such sadness.

Holy Spirit,
help me to surrender these dear ones to Jesus;
help me to surrender them completely to Him.

**"I know your pain, dear one.
It is not for you to carry.
Let go of it and give it to me…*all of it.*"**

I am pulling a heavy bag – it is full.
I am carrying so much.
The hurt - the pain - the sadness.

Then I stopped,
and I left it at the foot of the cross…
…and all the contents came falling out !

But now, they are all little flowers !
They are pouring out of the bag
- releasing such beauty - such joy

And the weight of all that
I had been carrying was gone…

Thank You, Father, God !

Praise You, Jesus !

***

*"Come to me all you who are heavy laden,
and I will give you rest".*
Matthew 11:28a

The Day God Spoke to Me

It was the end of the day, just on dusk.

And I was sitting in my garden
enjoying the quiet of the evening.

The birds had settled after a day of doing what birds do,
and an occasional night bird would break the coming silence
with a sound that echoed across the fading sky.

What a beautiful time of the day.

And I sat there – pensive – reflecting on what I had just seen.

I had been to see the movie "The Passion" and I was deeply moved by it.

As I sat in the garden my thoughts went to Jesus in the garden -
how He spent hours there, all alone, His three disciples falling asleep,
unable to stay awake and be there for Him.

He knew what was coming, what He was going to have to face.
He was going to have to stand, with my sin on Him
- and He was going to die for me, and for every person ever born.

As I sat there thinking about what He went through, what He did
– for **me** – and for everyone, the realization went deep into my heart,
into my spirit, of just how much He loved me …
… and how much He loves each one of us.

And I thought about how **His** Father must have felt as He sent His Son
to die for me - for all of us – and in such a horrific way.

I had believed this all of my life, but it was still hard to imagine
that He did it FOR ME, and at that moment, I just felt Him so near.

As I sat there in the quiet beauty of dusk, with the shades of the night
quietly descending, I heard a voice coming from a place in the sky
that I will never forget - a voice that said :

"I AM YOUR FATHER"

✲✲✲

I will be a Father to you.
2 Corinthians 6:18a

The Window in the Sky

We had just enjoyed such a great holiday.

He did not want to spoil it for me,
so he held on to it until we were back home.

Out of the blue, he said to me *"I have double vision"*.
Oh ! And I wondered with a check mark in my thoughts,

"What does that mean ?"

I wandered out onto the veranda
of our high set home, and looked up at the sky
that was full of stars and I quietly asked

"What is happening, God ?"

And as I looked, I saw something
that took my breath away.

I saw what looked like a window in the sky.
It was like an invisible window frame.

I couldn't explain it, but inside it
were three stars as bright as spotlights !
They outshone all the other stars in the sky.

I was stunned by this
and after a few moments, I looked away.

I looked again, and they were still there.

"What is this, God ?"

The brilliance of these few stars
filled the 'window' and it was unbelievable !

After a few minutes, I again looked away,
and then back again – *and they were gone.*

The sky was just its natural star-filled universe
that we see every night.

I stood there asking

"What are you telling me, LORD ?"

And I went back into the house wondering what lay ahead.

The cataracts in both eyes were removed,
and difficult thick glasses taking their place,
and that caused him to retire early from his job
as he couldn't see properly any longer.

This was very hard.

We worked through it
and had an early retirement,
along with educating our children.

6 years later he became ill,
and was diagnosed
with an untreatable cancer
and passed to Jesus in 2 months.

Again, it was hard, LORD,
especially on the children.

God had been there
in that miraculous window
to let us know that He was with us.

And He got us through.

How great is our God !

He is with us
in every moment of our lives.

And He has a plan
and a purpose
for each one of us.

Never give up !

***

"For I know the plans I have for you," declares the LORD,
*"plans to prosper you and not to harm you,
plans to give you hope and a future."*
Jeremiah 29:11 (NIV)

God's Army

While we praise Almighty God and give Him all the glory,
we are also in a constant battle with an enemy
who wants to pull us away from Him
and drag us into his pit.

God has given us what we need
to stand strong against this.

Being in the place and times of these days,
we need to use every weapon that we have been given. ..

Every person has been given at least one gift by the Holy Spirit.

This gift, whether a miracle, a word, an act of giving, or a hug,
are all weapons that go right into the face of the enemy,

Every gift from God is an arrow,
going straight into Satan and his hordes.

Our arrows go deep as people are raised up in prayer,
using every awesome gift that He has given us.

This is why we need to know – find out
– and then use, what we have been given.

We are in a major battle, and we need to be awake and aware
of all that is going on around us – and in our midst.

The battle for 'today's world' is real.

We all need to be fully dressed in our spiritual armour,
and we stand with a sword in our hand.

God has given us all the weapons
and the ammunition that we need.

We need to use them !

✸✸✸

*"Therefore take up the whole armour of God,
that you may be able to withstand in the evil day,
and having done all to stand."*
Ephesians 6:13
(continue to read verses 14 – 17)

Rumbling Hooves

I hear rumbling in the heavens
– it is like a roaring stampede
- but somehow staying in one place.

The roar is getting louder
– it is hooves – horses – stallions – war horses.

Straining for battle !

"It is not time," He says.

"The world is not ready for Me yet.

The day will come when I reach out for My loved ones
and will put them behind Me
- in a place of safety - a waiting place.

"Nations will fall - leaders will fear
- and turn in their fear.

But those leaders who know Me
will be raised up to fight a battle
- such as has never been seen before.

And they will be lifted up
and taken out of the way before
I bring My hand down."

PREPARE !

PREPARE THE WAY !

✳✳✳

*Now the number of the army of horsemen
was two hundred million;
And thus I saw the horses in the vision … "*
Revelation 9:16a-17a

*Then we who are alive and remain shall be caught up
together with them in the clouds to meet the Lord in the air.
And thus we shall always be with the Lord.*
1 Thessalonians 4:17

Part 5

Hope

The Winds of Faith

Father God, You breathed into the form of Adam ...

... and You gave him life.

No, it wasn't just a quiet, gentle, loving breath.
It was also the roar of a wind of life
that began with that first breath,
and has continued nonstop throughout
the world that was, that is, and that is to come.

It was an orchestrated wind of faith, hope, and love
that combats the wild winds of hopelessness, pain, and hate.

The eye of this cyclonic storm in the heavens
is a place of peace, restoration, and joy,
where we rest in His presence, and where
we can take time to breathe in the midst of the storm.

These are the moments when He tells us to stop
– to step back, rest, and listen for His voice above the storm ...

... until it is time for us to again, go into the storms of life
and battle, armed with the mighty breath of life He has given us.

It is also a mighty breath of love that goes through a dark world,
a world that is filled with hopelessness and hate and pain,
His breath coming in the roar of victory of the cross
and release from the chains of darkness
– a victory of love over hate – and of healing over pain.

It is our faith in Almighty God that overcomes the storms in our lives.
And it is the combined winds of faith, hope, and love, through
the sacrifice of the Lord Jesus Christ, that overcomes
the darkness of this world and brings the shining glory of God into it.

Hallelujah !

***

*He that dwells in the secret place of the most high,
shall abide in the shadow of the Almighty.*
Psalm 91:1

The Rock of Hope

Do not fear !

You are not going to be swept up that beach
and get bashed by incoming waves !

You are going to be set firmly on this Rock
– withstanding all that life tries to hit you with.

You have a strength that you do not realise.
A strength that is there for you every minute of every day.
It is holding you up, holding you steady, holding **you** !

And it is this strength that gives you hope to withstand
all that is thrown at you in this lost world that we live in.

Things have been so hard.

You are in deep water and the waves are pounding.
The pull of them is more than you can handle.

But there is a Rock standing high and safe in the sea
and you reach out to it and take hold as the ocean waves
seek to take you back and throw you on the beach.

They try again and again to grab you and carry you back
to its depths - and then the storm subsides.

You are exhausted and weary - but you are safe !

You were reaching out and clinging to the Rock
that never moves - He is always there for you to turn to
when the storms of life batter you, and toss you to and fro.

You think *"I can't do this"*
- while at the same time, Jesus Christ,
who is that Rock, has a hold of you
- and He is not going to let you go.

Jesus is greater than the one
who tries to get us to let go of this Rock.

It is a losing battle for him.

His strength is nothing compared to that of God.

The storms and raging waters of life
may try to toss and turn us,
but we stand safely and calmly on that Rock,
watching the waters swirling around
trying to reach us - but they cannot !

We are safe !

We are standing on the Rock.

Jesus is always there.

He is our Rock.

He is our Hope.

He is God.

Cling to Him.

He will never let go of you.

***

*The LORD is my rock,
my fortress, and my Saviour,
My God is my rock,
in whom I find protection.
He is my shield,
the power that saves me
and my place of safety.*
Psalm 18:2 (NLT)

Two Pieces of Wood

Two pieces of wood.

They are nothing.
Just sawn-down trees.

Jesus was a carpenter.

He could have been something else,
but His earthly father, Joseph,
chose to have his son be a carpenter.

It was God's plan for Jesus
to take pieces of wood,
and to turn them into things of use
- furniture - houses themselves.

He would have carved toys for children.

He took something that had stood
for many years, bringing beauty to those
who walked under its leafy branches,
cut it down, and transformed it
into useful items for people, and joy for children.

And it was this that God chose for His Son,
to sacrifice His life for us – for you and for me.

They took 2 pieces of wood – not beautifully carved,
but wood hewn into rough pieces - not sanded, but rough,
with spurs of splinters covering them.

One long and narrow, the other the same, but shorter.

They took a carpenter's tool and nailed
these two pieces of wood together and made a cross.

Two pieces of wood are what God the Father
had chosen for His beloved Son to be crucified on for you,
with nails pounded through His hands and His feet,
cruelly joining Him to these 2 pieces of wood.

His body screamed out in agony as they dropped
this wood into a hole in the ground, with splinters
tearing into the already cut-open flesh of His body.

This wood that once gave beauty
became an instrument of torture,
as they took a vine with spikes,
and made a crown of thorns
that was pressed into His head.

It is here our Lord and Saviour
hung for you- for us - because of our sin.
He took our sin onto His scourged body
– and looked up at His Father and cried out :

*"Father, forgive them,
for they know not what they do."*

And then He died.

Why are there often crosses,
2 pieces of wood, in churches ?

Because they forever remind us
of what Jesus did
– and that because of them,
we will one day be with Him
in our heavenly home.

Forever.

***

*...our Lord Jesus Christ
who gave Himself for our sins.*
Galatians 1:3b-4

The Waters of Redemption

Jesus, You are the fountain of life.

Of our life - waters of life erupting
- forever flowing from this fountain.

A fountain that has chips in it
– chunks torn out – and scratches
- yet, a vessel that carries perfect,
pure water to us all.

It is water that refreshes,
and restores all that has dried up.

Water that blesses, that heals, that forgives.

Waters that have REDEEMED us.

Waters that never run dry.

A fountain that carries the pain,
the ultimate sacrifice,
that You, Jesus Christ,
paid for us.

It is the fountain that carries
the waters of Redemption.

***

*In Him
we have redemption
through His blood.*
Ephesians 1:7

*I will give
of the fountain
of water of life
freely to him
who thirsts.*
Rev.21:6

Two Gardens

There are two gardens – God's garden and our garden.

We know about God's Garden of Eden.
He made this garden just for us.
But when Adam and Eve lost it, we lost it too.

One day we will again be there - with God.
But while we wait for that time to come,
He gives us another garden - our own
 - one that we plough and plant and dig and dig some more.

What do we start out with ?

A field that is neglected, overgrown with weeds – definitely unloved.

But as we look at it, we see it with new eyes.
We see it through His eyes as well as our own
 - our natural eyesight and our spiritual insight.

And so, I find my plot of forsaken beauty – empty and bare,
and I begin to toil with great expectation.

> *"This won't be hard, God !*
> *Look how I handle this mattock.*
> *This is easy."*

Bit by bit I dig into little bits that often become big bits !
Large rocks stuck in years-old clay and dirt.

I need to get these out, Lord;
they are blocking what I want to do.

These things that have been in my way for too long
 – kept me from getting through, because
I have started to think " I can't get rid of them".

So every day, it takes all my strength to say " GET LOST !"…
… and I get rid of these things that take up time.

Gone !
They are gone.
Hallelujah !

I take a moment after ridding myself of those tiresome
good-for-nothings, and look for what comes next.

And what do I see ?
Not just dirt and clay.

I see soil !

It is getting harder.
And I am getting hungry and thirsty.
I don't know if I can do this.
Help me, Lord !

You said I should take and eat, and I admit
my soul longs for You in this thirsty land.

Help me, Father.
"My child, I am sending you a helper.
It is My own Holy Spirit.
He will be there for you."

So I take out all the 'not needed', and 'not wanted'.
All that keeps me from spending time with You.

No fruit comes from weeds.

And all at once, my weedy space is clean and empty and waiting…
… and I am ready for the next step.

For the good stuff.

Fertilizer ! It makes the soil healthy
and ready for seeding and/or planting.

The fertilizer is the daily Word,
preparing the soil of my heart.
Sometimes it makes me look closer,
as I realize I have missed something,
or have done the wrong thing.

Then soon, all is ready, and I begin to seed
my space, my garden, by spreading Your Word,
and the garden of my thoughts with new growth, new life.

I dance between the rows of this new life I see coming to me
 - on both sides of me, in front of me, yes, even behind me.
The Holy Spirit rains down spring rains all year long.
I'm holding back as the times of waiting come – impatient
 – yet knowing all is in Your timing, Father God.

Then, time to fertilize again with the Word that encourages
and strengthens the changes that I feel, that I sense are coming.

All at once, it is in season, and there are shoots of green growth
that I see, that are beginning to show after 'hiding' all this time.

Praise God !

It has been such a long, hard but exciting journey, Holy Spirit.

And as I watch I see the green shoots turning into stems and leaves
that pridefully hold up the beautiful, multi-coloured flowers that
are coming up all through the garden.

Oh ! How beautiful they are - becoming a living, praising
garden of flowers of all shapes, sizes, and scents.

But wait ! What is that ?

Some of these have been chewed at, and some even totally eaten.
Oh, LORD, what have I done that has allowed this to happen ?

"Don't fear, My child. The enemy will try to discourage you,
but his threats are but like a bad smell. Do not give him any time,
just tend to your garden as he is not able to stop My Word
from spreading from your garden to all those who pass by.
Keep on doing as you are. He cannot harm you.
You are the keeper of this garden.
And you are under My covering protection.

Know that YOU ARE Mine !"

***

The LORD God planted a garden eastward in Eden.
Genesis 2:8a

Trust in the LORD with all your heart,
and He shall direct your paths.
Proverbs 3:5a, 6b

Hope in the Middle of the Storm

After spending a day with a friend who was dealing
with a difficult situation, I joined the traffic along the highway
that afternoon, the weather relentless with driving rain.

Driving along the coast road, I glanced seaward and saw a double rainbow.

When I got to a small seaside village, I drove to a look-out to see it in full
and a sight greeted me and made me stand in awe of God's hand.

The sky was dark with threatening clouds reflecting on a steel grey ocean.

And in front of me was the most brilliant rainbow I had ever seen.

The ends of this glowing semi-circle were aflame with each colour as they
dipped into the ocean, their radiance being painted across the dark water.

I was in awe of this beauty.

Then as I turned around to continue my drive the depth of the ocean
was replaced by a breathtaking vision in the distance.

In this dark sky, it looked as though a piece had been carved out of it,
leaving an empty space of the clearest ice blue – literally pristine in colour.

And in the very middle of this, stood the peak of a great mountain.

There was a beautiful white cloud that seemed to frame the top of the space;
not a fluffy white cloud, but one that looked as if God had taken a white
marker and drew a line along the pristine border, edging it perfectly.

As I looked at this awesome picture, it showed me that God is always
in the storm. We are never alone no matter how dark it seems.

His beauty, and His presence, are always there.

We are never alone.

***

"..so I will be with you;
I will never leave you or forsake you"
Joshua 1:5b (NIV)

Father, I am Home – Yay !

Psalm 24:1-2 says :

The earth is the LORD'S, and all its fullness,
The world and those who dwell therein.
For He has founded it upon the seas
and established it upon the waters.

Many have sung the song
"He's got the whole world in His hands."

So, let's take a look at this world - at the earth,
for a moment - in a very different way.

Look at what we do have.

We have oceans, deserts, mountains, jungles,
ice and snow, tropics, wide open spaces, and crammed cities.

We have dry, wet, hot, cold, and everything in between.

Now place a *small* round marble in the palm of *your* hand
and look at it as our world. We can't even begin to imagine it.

> *But God !*

So, regarding our earth and everything that it is,
we might just ask - what exactly *is* it ?

What is it made from, and how ?

It is full, empty, above, below, inside, outside and all mentioned above.

And we have the perfect Architect and Builder in our own space
amid this awesome Universe that He has given us to be part of.

He is virtually holding us in the palm of His hand !

But what is our earth made of and how does it work ?

Think about Him and about this :
the whole earth is being timed and orchestrated by Him !

He has also given us minds and imaginations
as we try to figure some of this out.

And He has given us His Holy Spirit to take us on the wonderful
and yes, at times crazy journeys to reveal to us Who our God is…

… and just who *we* are.

Like, with our amazing imagination seeing things such as this !

Under a covering of clouds, I see what looks like a huge round machine
with pieces and parts…all shapes, sizes, and colours … grinding, scraping,
clanging, going in different ways yet in full coordination as it manoeuvres
around in the reserved space and time in His universe.

What is all the clanging and noise ?

> *That is the sin we carry with us.*

But He takes it and turns it into beauty as we come to Him
every day of our life, repenting and following Him.

Everything works together, bringing His glory to us in the beauty
of love and forgiveness that we see in our daily lives.

The grinding and clanging become less and less, as we work with Him.

He is the designer of this world, this temporary home for His children,
until the day comes when Jesus takes us away to the unbelievable mansions
He planned for us since that very first moment of time.

This twisting highway of His plan for us is here until we reach the finish
line that is at the base of a beautiful ladder, topped with a massive white gate
with Gabriel or another like him there to welcome us.

God, the Father, has been preparing us to be His Son's bride, and to live
for Eternity in His presence. And to be with Jesus, to come to our very
own mansion, a 'home' envisioned by Him as a wedding gift to us.

It will be a home with no clanging, just chimes, bells, songs of glory, laughter, angels dancing on the roof, beauty everywhere, and Jesus' love reflecting **His** beauty throughout in the rays of the pure facets of a glistening white diamond, a jasper, that shines from Him.

His love and joy and beauty are everywhere !

And we bow in praise and awe before the throne of the awesome God, the Creator of all !

And then we look up at Him,
seeing what our heart believed,
and with love in our eyes, we say :

"Father, I am Home !

Yay !"

***

*"I will be
a Father to you,
and you shall be
My sons and daughters,"
says the LORD Almighty.*
2 Corinthians 6:18

www.ingramcontent.com/pod-product-compliance
Lightning Source LLC
Chambersburg PA
CBHW031301290426
44109CB00012B/682